Bookclub-in-a-Box presents the discussion guide for Abraham Verghese's novel
Cutting For Stone

Published in paperback by Vintage Canada, a division of Random House, Toronto 2010. Original copyright, 2009.

ISBN: 978-0-307-35778-6

Quotations used in this guide have been taken from the text of the paperback edition. All information taken from other sources is acknowledged.

This discussion companion for *Cutting For Stone* has been prepared and written by Marilyn Herbert, originator of Bookclub-in-a-Box. Marilyn Herbert, B.Ed., is a teacher, librarian, speaker, and writer. Bookclub-in-a-Box is a unique guide to current fiction and classic literature intended for book club discussions, educational study seminars, and personal pleasure.

This guide was co-written by Carol Verburg. For more information about the Bookclub-in-a-Box team, visit our website.

Bookclub-in-a-Box discussion companion for Cutting For Stone

(PRINT) ISBN 13: 978-1897082652
(E-PUB) ISBN 13: 978-1897082669
(E-PDF) ISBN 13: 978-1897082676

This guide reflects the perspective of the Bookclub-in-a-Box team and is the sole property of Bookclub-in-a-Box.

©2010 - DE - BOOKCLUB-IN-A-BOX - TORONTO, CANADA

Unauthorized reproduction of this book or its contents for republication in whole or in part is strictly prohibited.

CONTACT INFORMATION: SEE BACK COVER.

BOOKCLUB-IN-A-BOX
Abraham Verghese's Cutting For Stone

READERS AND LEADERS GUIDE . 2

INTRODUCTION

    Novel Quickline 7

    Key to the Novel, Setting . . 8

    Author Information 11

    Background Information 13

        Ethiopia 13

        Eritrea 14

        Carmelite Order 17

        Saint Teresa 18

        Saint Thomas 19

CHARACTERIZATION

    Names 23

        Sister Mary Joseph Praise 24

        Thomas Stone 24

        Marion, Shiva 25

        Hema 25

        Ghosh 26

        Genet, Rosina, Zemui . . .27

        Others 28

FOCUS POINTS AND THEMES

    Cutting for Stone 34

    Conjoinment, Separation . .34

    Love, Betrayal 36

    Belonging, Foreignness 37

    Missing 39

    Challenge, Fear, Courage . .40

    Teams, Individuals 41

    Regret, Redemption 42

WRITING STYLE AND STRUCTURE

    Narration 47

    Framing Device 48

    Plot 48

    Style 49

SYMBOLS

    Blood 50

    Stone 51

    Dance 52

    Holes 53

    Transplant 53

    Slippers 54

LAST THOUGHTS

    Healing vs. Curing 59

    Suggested Beginnings 60

FROM THE NOVEL (QUOTES) . . .67

ACKNOWLEDGEMENTS 77

BOOKCLUB-IN-A-BOX

Readers and Leaders Guide

Each Bookclub-in-a-Box guide is clearly and effectively organized to give you information and ideas for a lively discussion, as well as to present the major highlights of the novel. The format, with a Table of Contents, allows you to pick and choose the specific points you wish to talk about. It does not have to be used in any prescribed order. In fact, it is meant to support, not determine, your discussion.

You Choose What to Use.

You may find that some information is repeated in more than one section and may be cross-referenced so as to provide insight on the same idea from different angles.

The guide is formatted to give you extra space to make your own notes.

How to Begin

Relax and look forward to enjoying your book club.

With Bookclub-in-a-Box as your behind-the-scenes support, there is little for you to do in the way of preparation.

Some readers like to review the guide after reading the novel; some before. Either way, the guide is all you will need as a companion for your discussion. You may find that the guide's interpretation, information, and background have sparked other ideas not included.

Having read the novel and armed with Bookclub-in-a-Box, you will be well prepared to lead or guide or listen to the discussion at hand.

Lastly, if you need some more 'hands-on' support, feel free to contact us.

What to Look For

Each Bookclub-in-a-Box guide is divided into easy-to-use sections, which include points on characters, themes, writing style and structure, literary or historical background, author information, and other pertinent features unique to the novel being discussed. These may vary slightly from guide to guide.

INTERPRETATION OF EACH NOVEL REFLECTS THE PERSPECTIVE OF THE BOOKCLUB-IN-A-BOX TEAM.

Do We Need to Agree?

THE ANSWER TO THIS QUESTION IS NO.

If we have sparked a discussion or a debate on certain points, then we are happy. We invite you to share your group's alternative findings and experiences. You can contact us via our website (www.bookclubinabox.com), by email (info@bookclubinabox.com), or by phone (1-866-578-5571). We would love to hear from you.

Discussion Starters

There are as many ways to begin a book club discussion as there are members in your group. If you are an experienced group, you will already have your favorite ways to begin. If you are a newly formed group or a group looking for new ideas, here are some suggestions.

- Ask for people's impressions of the novel. (This will give you some idea about which parts of the unit to focus on.)
- Identify a favorite or major character.
- Identify a favorite or major idea.
- Begin with a powerful or pertinent quote. (Not necessarily from the novel.)
- Discuss the historical information of the novel. (Not applicable to all novels.)
- If this author is familiar to the group, discuss the range of his/her work and where this novel stands in that range.
- Use the discussion topics and questions in the Bookclub-in-a-Box guide.

If you have further suggestions for discussion starters, be sure to share them with us and we will share them with others.

Above All, Enjoy Yourselves

INTRODUCTION

Novel Quickline

Key to the Novel

Author Information

Background Information

INTRODUCTION

Novel Quickline

When Thomas Stone describes the *"cavernous tangle of blood vessels in the cortex"* (p.634) of his son Shiva's brain, he could be describing the story of his family and, in turn, this novel. Like the cerebral cortex itself, this story draws power from the intricate, convoluted way it folds in and out and over itself.

Characters appear, disappear, and reappear in new contexts; a seemingly minor incident may change everything, while an apparent catastrophe seems to change nothing. Since the narrator, Dr. Marion Praise Stone, is writing as a surgeon at Missing Hospital in Addis Ababa, Ethiopia, where he was born fifty years ago, we know at least part of his story's outcome. Yet the fast-paced plot remains suspenseful right up to the end. What we don't know is why Marion needs to *"heal the rift that separates my brother and me"* by telling their story. (p.9)

His starting point is his own and his brother's unexpected birth, which kills their mother, a nun. The babies' presumed father, Missing Hospital's chief surgeon, panics and disappears.

Another doctor, Hema, cuts the *"short fleshy tube"* (p.115), joining the twins at the head, revives them, and brings them up in partnership with Missing's remaining surgeon, Ghosh. The ripples from political events at the palace of Emperor Haile Selassie often rock the hospital compound and those around it. Like ShivaMarion (as the twins think of themselves), their country is growing up. When Marion is accused of involvement in the Eritrean rebellion, he must flee to the United States. There his path crosses his missing father's, and overlaps again with Shiva's. The novel's themes of insider vs. outsider, connection vs. separation, and love vs. betrayal re-erupt to pull the scattered family together in a life-and-death climax.

Key to the Novel

The Setting

A hospital

- A hospital is a crossroads for birth and death, injury and healing. Almost all of this novel takes place in and around two hospitals: first, Missing Hospital in Addis Ababa, then Our Lady of Perpetual Succour in the Bronx, New York. (see Missing, p.39)

- Missing Hospital is also the intersecting point between science and religion — both the Christian religion of its founders, and the traditional local beliefs of many of its African patients and staff.

    > *"... the commonest complaint in the outpatient department was "Rasehn...libehn...hodehn," literally, "My head...my heart...and my stomach ... this was how stress, anxiety, marital strife, and depression were expressed in Ethiopia ... psychic distress was projected onto a body part, because culturally it was the way to express that kind of suffering."* (p.157)

The single cure-all for their ailments, an injection, left the patients feeling better immediately.

A community

- The people in and around Missing know each other well. They feel connected by birth and geography — even though most of the people who work at the hospital are not native Ethiopians.

- Paths cross throughout the novel not only by coincidence, but because these people feel a shadow of the same kind of innate connection and interdependence that links ShivaMarion.

  We come unbidden into this life, and if we are lucky we find a purpose beyond starvation, misery, and early death which, lest we forget, is the common lot. (p.6)

- Various characters live on or near the hospital grounds and have arrived there for different reasons. For example, Almaz, Ghosh's housekeeper, had come for medical help. She believed she was pregnant and when her condition proved to be a uterine fibroid, she was ashamed to return home. She *"became one of the Missing People."* (p.138)

- In addition to Matron, the hospital's director, and the doctors, the other Missing People include Gebrew, the self-appointed watchman; Rosina, Hema's housekeeper and her daughter, Genet; Adam, the one-eyed diagnostician; W.W. Gonad, the lab technician; and the probationer. They are each close at hand when trouble erupts.

- When someone leaves the Missing community, they never forget it. Tsige was a young mother whose baby died. It was Marion, the child, who sat with her while she grieved, a kindness Tsige forever remembers. When Tsige moves to America, she continues her connection with fellow Ethiopians who come to Boston. She is especially delighted when Marion appears.

- A similar sense of community fills the halls of Our Lady of Perpetual Succour in the Bronx. This hospital's collection of characters includes Lou Pomeranz, the caretaker and self-appointed head of the hospital; B.C. Ghandi, doctor and cricket fan; Deepak Jesudass, chief resident; and a number of others who come from mostly East Indian cities. The key to membership in this community is to play, or at least cheer for, the game of cricket.

- At Missing, there was a handful of doctors who took on all medical problems that came through the door. At Our Lady of Perpetual Succour, there was no head doctor, save for the legendary Dr. Abramovitz who was too old and ill to do the job properly. The care of the patients fell to the residents and other assistants. Just as they did at Missing, these hospital workers salvaged the poor, the traumatized, and the disadvantaged. Marion feels right at home.

A Country

- The novel is infused with a strong sense of country, primarily of Ethiopia. This part of the setting takes up three-quarters of the novel. The reason is obvious – the place in which one is born, has family, makes friends, and experiences culture is the place that influences one's development. That stays with you even if you leave it forever. We see this with Marion, Tsige, and Abraham Verghese.

- In Ethiopia, Marion was created and divided, so it is fitting that Marion lives in two countries. He finds commonality in both places – birth, death, illness, and injuries. Because of the lack of resources, he is asked to deal with them in similar ways, with a figurative hand tied behind his back.

- But when Marian moves to the U.S., he is surprised by the sharp contrast in attitude towards issues of life and death: "*It was as if in*

Ethiopia, and even in Nairobi, people assumed that all illness—even a trivial or imagined one—was fatal; they expected death ... In America, my initial impression was that death or the possibility of it always seemed to come as a surprise, as if we took it for granted that we were immortal, and that death was just an option." (p.485, 486)

- The idea that death is the Missing culture's default assumption shows up in incidents ranging from the drowning of Koochooloo's puppies to Zemui's disappearance, as well as the motorcycle thief's expectation of killing anyone who gets in his way, and instead being killed himself.

- To understand and appreciate Verghese's very human novel, the setting is an important feature of focus.

Author Information

- **Personal history.** The author is a key to any novel; however, this novel is based more directly than most on the author's experience. Like three of his characters (Sister Mary Joseph Praise, Ghosh, and Hema), Verghese's parents were recruited from India to work in Ethiopia. There (like the Stone twins), their children were born and grew up. Like Thomas and Marion Stone, Verghese is a doctor who emigrated from Ethiopia to the United States.

- **Medicine.** As a physician, Verghese has enriched his novel with medical information and descriptions of medical procedures. His love of medicine also permeates the book, and was one reason he wrote it. He told an interviewer: *"I wanted to write about the sense a young boy has of the wonder of medicine and how it's some secret ritual that if you could only learn it, it's like buying X-ray spectacles and suddenly you could see through people."* (Brown)

- **Colorful settings**. In his rich descriptions of embarking from the docks in Madras, working at Missing Hospital, socializing in Addis Ababa, taking a first taxi ride through New York City, or discovering Boston, we can feel the author's affectionate delight in the places where he has lived — sometimes mixed with sorrow or frustration.

- Yet his sense of connection to his diverse homelands is tempered with the objectivity of a foreigner. As Verghese has remarked: *"Being a perennial outsider gives you a view, a way of seeing the world that has become almost a tic in my writing where I'm always looking on the outside in. Even when it is home."* (Brown)

- Abraham Verghese (pronounced 'ver-geese') was born in 1955 in Ethiopia. His parents were teachers from India's Kerala state, and Christians. On a visit there, the Ethiopian emperor Haile Selassie, also a Christian, was so impressed by the schools that when he opened his own schools back home, he recruited teachers from Kerala.

- Verghese grew up and was educated in Ethiopia. During medical school, he had to leave when the emperor was deposed and civil war broke out. After finishing his medical degree in Madras, India, he moved to the United States. He worked as a doctor in Tennessee, Boston, and Texas, and studied writing at the legendary Iowa Writers' Workshop. Unlike his characters, he is an internist, not a surgeon. As of 2007, he became a tenured professor and Senior Associate Chair for the Theory and Practice of Medicine at Stanford University, where he also has a writing office. In 2009, he became the director of the university's Internal Medicine Residency Program.

- *"Ethnically, I feel very much Indian. My parents are Indian ... But countrywise, I strongly identify with Ethiopia, having grown up there. And then of course, America ... is home unequivocally, and I am very proud to be American."* (Tadias)

- It was fiction that drew Verghese to become a doctor: first, W. Somerset Maugham's novel *Of Human Bondage*, which *"made medicine seem like a romantic passionate pursuit,"* (BookRabbit) and then the novels of physician A.J. Cronin and others. Verghese wrote a short story on AIDS for *The New Yorker*, which led to his first book, the non-fiction memoir *The Tennis Partner*. After a second non-fiction book, *My Own Country*, he returned to his first love, fiction, with *Cutting for Stone*.
- Abraham Verghese has been married twice and has three sons.

Background Information

Ethiopia

Emperor Haile Selassie, a powerful offstage figure in *Cutting for Stone*, was the last "King of Kings" to rule Ethiopia from the world's longest-lived monarchy. His royal line, the Solomonic Dynasty, is said to descend directly from the Biblical King Solomon and the Queen of Sheba.

Under his pre-coronation name, Ras (a title, sometimes translated as Prince) Tafari, Haile Selassie became the central figure of the Rastafarians in Jamaica (novel, p.130).

- Ethiopia is home to approximately 80 million people, with Addis Ababa as its capital. The population has nearly tripled since the timeframe of this novel.
- The country is landlocked, surrounded by Eritrea to north, Sudan to west, Somalia to east, Kenya to south.
- Ethiopia has been an identifiably independent nation dating back to ancient times. It is mentioned in the Bible in relation to the story of Solomon and Sheba, the Ethiopian Queen.

- It is the home of the coffee bean or berry known as "buna," which grows wild on plants in the forest regions. Arab travelers found it and carried it out of Ethiopia to other places. This is one account of the origin of coffee arabica. The drinking of coffee is a ritual that takes some time and is accompanied by snack food, such as popcorn.
- Ethiopia has been home to the world's three major religions. The country is predominantly Christian dating back to the 4th century, when the St. Thomas Christians came from Kerala, India to establish their church. One-third of the population is Muslim. The Muslims arrived in the 7th century from Mecca where they were undergoing persecution. Until about 1980, Ethiopia had a significant Jewish presence.
- A 2005 Unicef report states that 74% of all women undergo female circumcision. While in most regions of Ethiopia, this procedure is done at birth, in the regions of Amhara and Tigray, it is carried out either between the ages of seven and nine, or just before marriage between the ages of fifteen and seventeen. (see Genet, p.27)
- The literacy rate for men is approximately 50%. For women, the rate is around 35%.

Eritrea

- The area of Eritrea, sitting at Ethiopia's head, is also mentioned in ancient times, not as an autonomous state, but as an area whose name was given as the Erythrean Sea, referring to the Red Sea, on which it sits.
- In this way, Ethiopia and Eritrea can be viewed as having once been a single region; they were, in effect, conjoined. Despite this image, it is important to understand that the entire area was made up of countless numbers of small villages, often with their own languages, dialects, and cultural practices. It may sound confusing, but it

worked. In terms of the novel, this history is similar to the environment of both the Mission Hospital and Our Lady of Perpetual Succour, where people from many diverse backgrounds lived and worked together with similar purpose.

- In the middle of the 19th century, Italy, which had itself just become a united political entity, came looking for land on which to build an empire. They colonized around Asmara (where Rosina is from), and they built and developed vital urban, rural, and business infrastructures. It was the Italians who gave the area its political nametag – Eritrea. They liked being there, but they wanted more – control of Ethiopia.

- In 1889, Ethiopia was the only independent country in Africa, surrounded by British, French, and now Italian rulers. Menelik II was the self-proclaimed emperor. He came to the Italians with a treaty giving them political control over Eritrea in exchange for their recognition of his absolute rule over Ethiopia.

- The Italians agreed, but unfortunately, something was lost in the translation. The Amharic version read as Menelik wanted, but the Italian report stated that any foreign contract or business involving Ethiopia had to have Italian approval. With the stroke of a pen, the Italians became the virtual protectors of both areas, Eritrea and Ethiopia.

- Menelik objected and went to war in the famous Battle of Adwa that Ghosh describes on p.147, 148. Miraculously, Menelik won, but while Ethiopia stayed independent, the Italians remained in Eritrea. A virtual border was now in place, the first of several significant separations between the two areas.

- In 1930, Haile Selassie came to power, but in 1935, the Italians re-entered Ethiopia with Mussolini's help. This time, the Italians successfully seized Ethiopia. Selassie was deposed and fled to England where he appealed in vain for support from Britain and the League of Nations, of which Ethiopia was a member.

- It was only in 1941 that Britain and her allies decided to push Mussolini out of the entire area, thus allowing Selassie to return and annex Eritrea for his own purpose as a seaport.

- Despite this, many Italians stayed behind and continued to exert their influence while building up the country. As Hema observes, the Italians saw *"life for ... what it was – an interlude between meals"* (p.92) Nevertheless, they helped construct the city of Addis Ababa in grand European style, a place of contradiction. Ethiopia's capital city is a modern, cosmopolitan urban centre in a country where 83% of the residents are rural, 46% are under the age of 14, and, on average, 42% are illiterate.

- This brings us to the '60s and 70's, the timeset of the novel. Selassie was a great fan of education (see Author Information, p.11). Many of Ethiopia's students had gone abroad to study. They returned with many new ideas, such as the Marxist approach of giving power to the people. The threat of coup was in the air and while the army was deciding to stay loyal to the Emperor or overthrow him, the students took to the streets in the thousands. Even W. W. Gonad marched under the banner of the School of Business.

    > *My countrymen awake – history calls you*
    > *No more slavery, let freedom reign anew.*
    >
    > *Banners in English read:* FOR EVERYONE, A BLOODLESS REVOLUTION AND LET US STAND PEACEFULLY WITH THE NEW GOVERNMENT OF THE PEOPLE ...
    >
    > *... We learned later from W.W. Gonad that in the Merkato the Muslims and Eritrean shopkeepers received the students with cheers. But elsewhere in Addis, their reception by the public was cold ...* (p.290, 291)

- It was against this background that the Eritreans launched their efforts to gain independence from Ethiopia. They hadn't said much in the twenty years after the British drove out the Italians, but beginning around 1961, The Eritrean Liberation Front grew stronger.

- Someone like Genet, who was already confused by her place in the family, in her culture (Eritrean), and in her country of birth (Ethiopia), became very sensitive to current events. For example, Asmara, the crown jewel of Eritrea, was handed to Selassie by the British as punishment to the Eritreans for their collaboration with the Italians.

- The entire situation became an *"accidental consequence of history"* (p.39), much like the accident of birth that created Shiva and Marion. This was the beginning of a dance that engaged the two countries for years to come. (see Dance, p.52)

Use this short history of Ethiopia and Eritrea to connect Shiva, Marion, and Genet to the themes of connection, conjoinment, and separation.

Carmelite Order - Discalced Carmelites

- The Order of Discalced (or Barefoot) Carmelites represents the eremitic tradition of the Catholic Church. Inspired by the desert fasting of Jesus and his hermit cousin John the Baptist, members forsake the chaos and distraction of social communities for the stoicism of solitude. The original Order of the Brothers of Our Lady of Mount Carmel, or Carmelites, focused on contemplative prayer.

- In the 1560s, with that order and others losing ground, Teresa of Avila led a reform movement inspired by her own mystical experience. After much prayer and reflection, she set up a Carmelite convent where poverty and renunciation of property were the rule. She, John of the Cross, Anthony of Jesus, and others went on to found a series of similarly focused monasteries and convents in Spain and Italy.

- From there, they traveled through Persia to Goa, India where they established a number of missions and eventually sent representatives out into the world, Ethiopia included.

Saint Teresa

- Teresa Sánchez de Cepeda y Ahumada was born in 1515 in Ávila, Old Castile, Spain, and died in 1582 in Salamanca. She was fascinated from childhood by the lives of the saints. As a little girl she tried to run away with her brother to become a martyr. When adolescence distracted her, her father sent her to a convent school. Reading St. Jerome helped revive her piety, and she entered a Carmelite convent – at that time, not a very severe environment. Teresa's contemplation of Jesus's suffering on the cross led to her commitment to poverty and simplicity as the core of a religious life and the goal of her later reforms.

- Becoming chronically ill, Teresa began to experience religious ecstasies. Through prayer, contemplation, and reading the medieval mystics, she rose through stages to a perfect union with God.

- In *Cutting for Stone*, Sister Mary Joseph Praise emulates this practice of "contemplation, elevation, and ecstasy" during her missionary voyage from Madras to Aden. *"After ten hours ... [she] suddenly felt print and page dissolve; the boundaries between God and self disintegrated. Reading had brought this: a joyous surrender of her body to the sacred, the eternal, and the infinite."* (p.17)

- The print that Sister Mary Joseph Praise carries with her is of Bernini's famous statue depicting one of Teresa of Avila's ecstasies. An angel pierces her heart repeatedly with a flaming golden spear, filling her with pain and love for God.

Saint Thomas

- Thomas the Apostle was one of the twelve men chosen by Jesus as his closest followers. His nickname "Doubting Thomas" comes from his reaction when the other apostles reported seeing Jesus alive after his fatal crucifixion: Thomas refused to believe it unless he could see and feel for himself the nail and spear holes in Jesus's body. Later Jesus appeared to all the apostles and invited Thomas to satisfy himself.

- The Gospel According to John, where this Biblical story appears, refers to him as "Thomas called Didymus" – the Greek word for twin. The name Thomas comes from the Aramaic name Ta'oma, also meaning twin. In the "Gospel of Thomas" from Nag Hammadi, he is known as Didymos Judas Thomas; he might have been called the Twin to distinguish him from Judas Iscariot, or because (in another Nag Hammadi document) Jesus calls him "my twin and true companion."

- In *Cutting for Stone*, Sister Mary Joseph Praise is a Malayali Christian from the state of Kerala: *"Malalayi Christians traced their faith back to St. Thomas's arrival in India from Damascus in A.D. 52. 'Doubting' Thomas built his first churches in Kerala well before St. Peter got to Rome."* (p.15,16)

CHARACTERIZATION

Sister Mary Joseph Praise

Thomas Stone

Marion, Shiva

Hema, Ghosh

Genet, Rosina, Zemui

Others

CHARACTERIZATION

Names

- Although Verghese writes in English, few of his characters have English-language names. Still, many of the characters' names do have significant meanings for an English-speaking reader.

- Perhaps mindful of most readers' likely unfamiliarity with the languages his characters speak, Verghese has chosen names that are different enough for us to tell them apart readily, and familiar or simple enough for us to remember: Ghosh, Gebrew, Almaz, Zemui, Mebratu, Deepak, Tsige.

- Some of the longer and less familiar character names are abbreviated to memorable nicknames: Dr. Kalpana Hemlatha becomes Hema, Wonde Wossen Gonafer becomes W.W. Gonad, B.C. Gandhinesan becomes B.C. or Ghandi.

Sister Mary Joseph Praise

- Nuns generally choose their own names. Sister Mary Joseph Praise's name honors Mary, the mother of Jesus, and her husband, Joseph. Nuns vow to be celibate, and yet (like the Virgin Mary) Sister Mary Joseph Praise bore sons. Her missionary journey to Africa, like Mary and Joseph's journey to Bethlehem (where their son was born) was made under compulsion, and was followed by dangers to their offspring.

- Sister Mary Joseph Praise's Order of Discalced Carmelites has a particular veneration for the Virgin Mary.

- In spite of all her tribulations, Sister Mary Joseph Praise always focused on God's goodness, and presumably chose "Praise" as part of her name for that reason.

- The hospital, Our Lady of Perpetual Succour (the latter meaning "help in time of need"), is a Catholic reference to the Virgin Mary, who is often asked to ask Christ for help for the faithful. Marion, and others, use both the Virgin Mary and Sister Mary Joseph Praise for such intervention.

Thomas Stone

- Thomas Stone shares more than one connection with Saint Thomas. (see Saint Thomas, p.19) He refuses to believe the obvious truth, that his beloved Mary is dying in childbirth, until too late. At her death he wrestles with her faith. Then he turns his back on his own twins.

- Yet, in the pioneer footsteps of St. Thomas, Dr. Stone came to Ethiopia to bring healing — in his case, via faith in medical science rather than Christianity.

- His last name, Stone, ties in with the novel's title and central metaphor. (see Cutting for Stone, p.34) It also represents the split between faith and skepticism, true of medicine as well as religion.

Marion Praise Stone

- Marion is named by Hema, Missing Hospital's gynecologist, in honor and appreciation of Dr. Marion Sims (1813–1883), *"considered the father of obstetrics and gynecology."* (p.131)
- Since the name Marion is a variation of Mary, Hema is also naming the baby after his mother.

Shiva Praise Stone

- The Hindu god Shiva is the one Hema just invoked when her plane almost crashed. She calls on him again when she learns the twins are not stillborn: *"the god whom others thought of as the Destroyer, but who she believed was also the Transformer, the one who could make something good come out of something terrible."* (p.120)
- The god Shiva is also associated with dance. Hema thinks of this when she first rocks the twin babies. (p.129) Dance becomes important for Shiva Stone as he grows up. (see Dance, p.52)

Hema

- Hema is what everyone calls Dr. Kalpana Hemlatha. In medicine, "hema" is a Greek-derived prefix meaning blood. As Missing Hospital's gynecologist and obstetrician, Hema is very familiar with blood.

- Hematology is the branch of internal (and other areas of) medicine that concerns blood, the organs that make it, and the diseases that involve it — a specialty of Dr. Abraham Verghese.

- When the twins are born, and Hema takes over from Thomas Stone, she calls repeatedly for blood to transfuse into their dying mother. Then she must sever the fleshy stem that joins the babies' heads, which Stone must have torn while trying to deliver them: *"from this rent, what little blood the twin infants possessed was pumping out."* (p.115)

- Although Hema is the lifeblood of Ghosh and the boys, she has no blood relationship to them — she is not Marion and Shiva's birth mother.

Ghosh

- Ghosh is the only character in the novel whose given name we are never told. He is Dr. Ghosh to his patients and colleagues, but simply Ghosh to his friends and family. Ghosh is a common Hindu surname.

- And yet, Ghosh himself is anything but common. He is simultaneously larger than life and as cuddly as a small favored animal. He has so much body hair that Hema thinks of him as wearing a *"gorilla coat."* (p.52) His constant five o'clock shadow and his small pot-belly diminishes his physical stature, but his voice is boomingly loud and unavoidable. To Hema, and to all who love him, Ghosh is *"strangely beautiful."* (p.54)

- Where Hema is the lifeblood of the family and the novel, Ghosh is its head and heart. He is wise, witty, and intensely honest, so much so that his reach exceeds his physical life. His influence is felt even after his untimely death.

- Most importantly, he is Thomas Stone's friend. (see Redemption, p.42)

Genet, Rosina, Zemui

- Genet is the girl who grows up like a sister to the Stone twins. Her name is pronounced with a hard "g" and is a common Ethiopian name meaning "promise, Eden, paradise." We can imagine her mother, Rosina, naming her baby with such hope.

- Much of Genet's later difficulties comes as a result of her confused identity. Born just after Shiva and Marion, the three are raised and educated together. However much time Genet spends in Hema's house during the day, at night she goes back to the single room she shares with her Eritrean mother.

- Her father, Zemui, drives for Colonel Mebratu, an important man in the Imperial Bodyguard. Zemui comes often to the compound because he parks Mebratu's motorcycle there. When he does not stay to visit with Rosina, Zemui goes home to his wife and children. Genet is biologically outside the circle of real family, and physically outside Hema and Ghosh's family. Figuratively, Genet is outside the Ethiopian family as well.

- All of this plants seeds of confusion and destruction in Genet's mind. As Marion tells us, no one knew when Rosina was pregnant that she was *"carrying the seed of revolution"*: Genet. (p.225)

- Rosina's name is a variation of the common rose. While a rose is a thing of beauty, it carries sharp thorns on its stem. Rosina pricks Genet first by scarring her face and then by having Genet vaginally circumcised. Much later, Genet's blood flows into Marion and tragically creates havoc in his system. (see Blood, p.50)

Others

Matron

- Like Ghosh, Matron Hirst is known by her title rather than her name. She is the dignified supervisor and "mother" of all who come through Missing Hospital's doors. She needs no other label.

- But, like the other characters, Matron is a woman of contradictions. She was not always a nun in the pure sense of that role. She was also a woman who had once been in love, with a man named John Melly. In telling Ghosh about Melly, they have a discussion about faith and doubt, the thematic twin ideas of the novel. Matron tells Ghosh that *"doubt is a first cousin to faith ... to have faith, you have to suspend your disbelief."* (p.165) This juxtaposition applies to both religion and science, the helix of the book's hypothesis.

- Matron is the female counterpart to Ghosh's strong leadership. She creates medical miracles of a different kind — she truly makes something out of nothing. Her manipulation of the donations received from well-meaning donors is something to behold.

- Matron is God's gardener. She planted hope in Missing's patients, her staff, and supporters like Eli Harris. In the actual garden where Sister Mary Joseph Praise and her son are buried, Matron planted a flower that she herself had developed and registered: *the Rosa rubininosa Shiva*. The seeds that were planted so many years before grew into a new organization called The Shiva Stone Institute for Fistula Surgery, funded and supported by the once-missing Thomas Stone.

Probationer

- The young woman initially known only as the probationer, and then as the staff probationer, appears at key moments throughout *Cutting for Stone*. Her title implies that she plays a supporting role. However, she is intimately involved in many of the crucial incidents in the story.

- Like Rosina, the probationer has also come from Eritrea to make a new life. Her coming to Missing was an *"accident of history"* (p.39), like Eritrea's conjoinment with Ethiopia. (see Eritrea, p.14) In the probationer's case, the accident was a positive one because she received a scholarship to the nursing school at Missing Hospital. Given her personality and penchant for strictly following the rules of what she interprets as *"sound nursing sense,"* she constantly tempts *"fate to stick a foot out and trip her."* (p.40)

- However badly she messes up, her heart is in the right place. She forges ahead almost invisibly, and in the end, she finds her true position. She is Shiva's assistant and then becomes a confident surgeon who trains other doctors in fistula surgery.

- She has found her identity. On the book's next-to-last page, Marion learns her real name: Naeema, an Arabic name meaning "comfort."

Almaz

- Almaz is Ghosh's housekeeper and very occasional sexual partner. Her absolute loyalty reflects the meaning of her name: "diamond." The image of Almaz, family picture in hand, standing for every car that passes on its way in and out of the prison is one of powerful devotion. She wanted Ghosh to know that he was important and remembered. Ghosh did see her and this action was in fact what told him that the family was fine. He needed this comfort to keep going.

Mebratu

- Colonel Mebratu was a member of the Imperial Bodyguard, dedicated to protecting the emperor. Although he is likely involved in plotting to overthrow Selassie, Ghosh gives us a picture of this complex man.

- Ghosh once corrected Mebratu's twisted bowel and recalled seeing Mebratu orchestrate a public execution of others who were part of a similar plot. Mebratu told Ghosh those men were his friends, but he carried out the sentence because he believed he was doing the right thing at the time.

   > *"I sensed that," Ghosh said, recalling the strange dignity of both the executioner and the condemned.* (p.172)

- Much later, Ghosh is called to the palace to heal Mebratu's injuries, the result of a brutal beating, so that Mebratu could then be executed. Mebratu's executioner was equally a friend and colleague. The gaining of power is a circular struggle and Mebratu accepts his fate in the knowledge that, while many have died for this cause, others will carry on the task of trying to create his vision of a positive government for the people. *"I go to tell others the seed we planted has taken root."* (p.341)

Consider how each of the characters is a contradiction of terms. In what ways do they fit with the novel's themes and with Ethiopia's issues?

FOCUS POINTS AND THEMES

Cutting For Stone

Conjoinment, Separation

Love, Betrayal

Belonging, Foreignness

Missing

Personal Challenge, Fear, Courage

Teams, Individuals

Regret, Redemption

FOCUS POINTS AND THEMES

This novel's core theme is interconnectedness, an idea that applies to its many other themes and symbols as well as to its characters and plot lines. It also applies to Verghese's intertwined lines of work: "*Writing and medicine are not separate. My writing emanates from this stance that I take, looking at the world, and the stance is purely from being a physician — it's one of observing, cataloguing, being in wonder and awe of what I see.*"
[Blitzer]

To understand connection requires understanding its opposite, division. The paradox of linked opposites appears throughout this book. Themes are not only interlocked but sometimes contradictory. The biggest contradiction is life, which is full of mismatched concepts and inconsistencies. The first evidence of this is the novel's opening — a nun giving birth. This does of course happen, but by definition, it shouldn't. The fact that the boys survive belies all that accompanies the events of their birth.

Cutting for Stone

The book's title takes on different meanings as the story progresses.

- In the 5th century, Hippocrates wrote a list of promises that is recited by medical graduates to this day. The phrase *"cutting for stone"* is part of their promise not to perform invasive procedures on patients that go beyond their skill level. Hippocrates picked that particular point because kidney and bladder stones were common, but deadly ailments. Medical caregivers who did not know what they were doing would operate haphazardly and leave the patients to suffer and die from blood infections. (see Blood, p.50)

- Stone is the narrator's family name. He shares it with his father and twin brother. (See Thomas Stone, p.24) All three Stones are surgeons: their occupation is cutting. Other doctors in the novel cut literally for Dr. Stone, either to correct him (Hema and Ghosh when they try to save the Sister), under his instructions (Deepak and Marion in New York), or in spite of Thomas Stone. Shiva ends up repairing holes that parallel the one his father tried to make in his head when he was born.

- When Shiva Stone becomes an expert in fistula surgery, patients show up at Missing Hospital with a piece of paper that may say simply, in Amharic, CUTTING FOR STONE. (p.576)

- At the book's end we see each of the Stones use his surgical knowledge on behalf of the other two in a life-and-death operation.

Conjoinment and Separation

- As conjoined twins, Marian and Shiva are connected from the moment of conception, and they remain connected throughout their lives. Physically, however, the link between their heads must be cut in order for them to be born. After birth, they continue to sleep head-to-head whenever they can. As they grow up, sometimes they choose to part from each other, but they always come back together.

- When Shiva dies after donating part of his liver to save his twin's life, Marion struggles with the shock and grief of separation. Then he realizes: *"Shiva and I were one being: ShivaMarion ... By a brilliant and daring rearrangement of organs ... we had downsized to one ... One being at birth, rudely separated, we are one again."* (p.639, 640)

- The connection between the twins' nanny, Rosina, and her daughter, Genet, goes the other way. Rosina tries to stop Genet from separating from her as an adolescent. She literally blocks her daughter's blossoming sexuality by having Genet's vagina sewn up. The resulting infection almost kills Genet and spurs her to make a complete break from her mother. That leads Rosina, in despair, to a permanent separation: suicide.

- Birth separates the twins from their parents by death and desertion. Yet the connection is not lost, only stretched thin. Lacking parents, the babies prod Hema to quit resisting her bond with Ghosh, so that the four of them can become joined in an ad hoc family.

- Not only people tilt between connection and separation. Also conjoined are religion and medicine. Practitioners of each may try to keep them separate, but they intertwine nevertheless. Both require a similar kind of faith. When Sister Mary Joseph Praise is on her deathbed, and Thomas Stone can't save her with his surgical skills, he calls on *"a God he had renounced once and didn't believe in"* (p.122), hoping that her faith will triumph over his skepticism.

- Eritrea, conjoined with Ethiopia, is trying to separate, while Ethiopia is determined to hang on. Both countries already have gone through linking and disconnection with their European conquerors, Italy and Germany.

There are a great many examples and scenes of connection and separation. This is a good place to start a discussion of the novel's themes and their interconnectedness to each of the characters.

Love and Betrayal

- Love is one of the important bonds that links the novel's characters together, and betrayal is a counter-force which separates them. The most striking example is Genet's betrayal of Marion's love for her by seducing Shiva, which damages the bonds among all three of them.

- Thomas Stone learned as a child that love leads to betrayal and loss. As a result, he refuses to face his love for Sister Mary Joseph Praise. Because of this betrayal, he loses her.

- Stone also betrays his twin sons, but that broken bond spurs Hema to love the boys and create a family around them. When Marion finally meets his birth father, his sense of betrayal is stronger at first than love. Only when he understands how Thomas Stone's own father betrayed him can he start mending their tie.

- With Genet, too, Marion hopes that the way to overcome the pain of having been spurned by her is through love. He has waited his entire life for Genet to return. When she does, Marion acts out in rage and physically loses his virginity for the first time. Marion's sense of love and betrayal both unites and separates them for the last time.

- Once Marion knows Genet's entire story, he is able to separate from his all-encompassing love for her. He realizes that his love has turned to sympathy. This is a *"feeling better than love, because it released me, it set me free. Marion, I said to myself, she found her greatness, at last, found it in her suffering."* (p.601)

- Genet deserts Marion again, but Marion suffers even more than before. Genet gives him the illness that will cause his brother's death after it nearly kills him.

   The relationship between Marion and Genet defies common sense. Is it plausible that he could harbor such deep and misguided emotions for her for so long? Why did Genet go to see Marion this last time? Did she mean to do him harm?

Belonging and Foreignness

- What defines "home"? Most of Missing Hospital's staff came to Ethiopia from somewhere else, and in many ways they remain "ferengi" — foreigners. Stone is an Englishman born in India; Matron is from England. Hema, Ghosh, and Sister Mary Joseph Praise are from India. Rosina, Genet, and the Probationer are Eritreans. Marion, born in Addis Ababa of English and Indian parentage, emigrates to America, where he works with Indian doctors. As Hema returns from her birthplace to her workplace, she mulls the contrast: isn't home *"not where you are from, but where you are wanted?"* (p.95)

- She came to Ethiopia looking for a kind of belonging that was not connected to social definitions and injunctions. She knew that in India she could never achieve independence and stature as a doctor. In Addis, she felt valued.

    The city is evolving, and I feel part of that evolution, unlike in Madras, where the city seems to have been completed centuries before I was born. (p.94)

- The novel's central family, too, is linked not by blood but by need and desire. Until she takes custody of the twins, Hema has refused to marry Ghosh, partly because of the differences in their social class and partly because she had a foolishly romantic notion of love, one that came out of the British novels that she read as a child. She won't commit to him for more than a year at a time in order to keep the connection fresh and alive.

- Although Marion and Shiva grow up treating Ghosh and Hema as their parents, they know they also belong to the late Sister Mary Joseph Praise and the departed Thomas Stone. Marion particularly feels the sting of the cut that their disappearance left.

- Genet's sisterly role in their family changes at puberty, creating confusion as to who belongs with whom and in what ways.

- Politically, belonging to the right group can be literally a matter of life and death. The emperor's government hunts Col. Mebratu at one point as a traitor, and later embraces him. Genet is Eritrean from birth, but when she becomes a separatist rebel, even Marion as her friend is branded a dangerous foreigner. Fleeing Ethiopia through Eritrea, he is helped by his homeland's so-called enemies.

- In America, Marion is one among many foreign medical students who are united by two common activities: providing care to New York City's poor, and playing cricket. *"After just a week in the hospital, I felt I'd left America for another country ... where more than half the citizens spoke Spanish. When they spoke English it wasn't what I expected in the land of George Washington and Abraham Lincoln."* (p.476)

- The novel's medical setting extends the image of foreignness versus belonging to human organs. Shiva is able to save his brother's life by donating part of his liver as a transplant. Because they are twins, Marion's immune system won't reject Shiva's liver as foreign.

Missing

- A language misunderstanding leads to Mission Hospital being renamed Missing Hospital by its Ethiopian hosts. Once it was written on the page, it was as if the name were carved in stone.

- Both names are apt. Many of the characters pursue a mission: to save souls, to save lives, to find redemption for their own or someone else's past mistakes. However, their original mission or purpose is often lost or changed by events, and therefore is missing from all that follows.

- The novel draws suspense from the quests of its diverse characters, and their endless longing to find or replace what is missing:
  - Mothers, fathers, dead and dying babies are grieved and missed
  - Thomas Stone disappears and is missing from his sons' lives until they reach adulthood. He is missed by Marion, who finally tracks him down in America.
  - Genet fiercely resents her father for abandoning her and her mother, until he disappears completely. Then she devotes herself to his memory.
  - Sister Mary Joseph Praise's Aden story is missing — we never learn what terrible things happened to her there.
  - Thomas Stone's personality has missing pieces, some of which surface when he loses the woman he didn't realize he loved.
  - Stone is also missing a finger, which he amputated himself and which Sister Mary Joseph Praise kept in a jar.
  - Missed opportunities lead some characters into lifelong regrets: Stone missed the chance to share love with Sister Mary Joseph Praise, and then with their sons. Genet missed out on the love Marion offered her, and Marion passed up sexual opportunities with Genet, Tsige, and the probationer.

- Money is often missing. There are insufficient funds for the hospitals in both Ethiopia and the U.S. to provide good care, and for individuals to take good care of themselves and their loved ones.
- Sterilized equipment is usually kept in a hospital's autoclave room. Since there was a scarcity of such supplies at Missing, the room's purpose changed. Sister Mary Joseph Praise kept a small desk and chair there at which Marion often sat unobserved.
- The man who steals Zemui's motorcycle is missed by his brother, but he is never found.
- Ghosh's symptoms are missed or overlooked by all those around him, until they become fatally obvious.

• The things that are missing leave gaping holes. (see Holes, p.53)

Personal Challenge, Fear, Courage

• Personal challenge is the goal of each of the characters. Fear is an obstacle in their paths; courage is their weapon. Personal challenge is also the essence of faith in both religion and in medicine.

• Matron tells Marion to do the hardest thing he can imagine, so he chooses surgery. Her point, which he accepts, is that personal challenge is the only way to progress beyond what is easy and comfortable to a full use of one's gifts.

• One of Ghosh's favorite sayings, quoted by Marion and other characters, is the famous line, *"Screw your courage to the sticking-place, and we'll not fail!"* In Shakespeare's play Macbeth, Lady Macbeth's goal was to shame her husband into carrying out their plan to murder their king. There are various theories as to exactly what a sticking-place is, but the point is clear: get a strong enough grip on yourself to conquer your fears, and success is assured.

- Sister Mary Joseph Praise, in meeting the challenge to carry God's love to Africa, overcame fear (including a horrific experience in Aden) and completed her journey to Missing Hospital. There, refining her love for God and laboring in his service, she came to love Thomas Stone.

- Thomas Stone's challenge was to avoid loving another human being for fear of betrayal and loss. He ended up loving, betraying, and losing Sister Mary Joseph Praise. Much later, he was able to find the courage to tell his son Marion about his fear, and accept the chance to love his children.

- Marion set himself the challenge of winning Genet. Although he pursued his goal courageously, he ended up losing Genet to Shiva and losing Shiva to Genet (although not in the usual sense).

Teams and Individuals

- In most of this novel's settings, whether household or hospital, teamwork is crucial. Individuality, so highly prized in many American novels, is often dangerous here. Thomas Stone is a brilliant surgeon and the star of Missing Hospital, but he falls apart when he has to deliver Sister Mary Joseph Praise's babies alone It was his refusal to acknowledge his bond with her that led to her secret pregnancy and her death.

- Hema recognizes immediately that any chance of saving Sister Mary Joseph Praise depends on teamwork. She and Stone must deliver the babies together, and others must give blood. *"Time and time again, she and Ghosh and Stone and Matron would donate their own blood and prevail on some of the nurses to do the same."* (p.106)

- With their mother dead and their father fled, the babies need some other family to survive. Hema steps in, and overcomes her qualms about marrying Ghosh, to save the twins and also herself: *"These two babies plugged a hole in my heart that I didn't know I had until now."* (p.130) As the saying goes, it takes a village to raise a child: the Missing community moved literally into Hema's house and took up residence. While Matron stayed only for a while, Rosina and Almaz worked together as a team to look after the new family.

- Political power depends on the number and strength of one's supporters. The emperor may call himself the king of kings or a god or whatever he likes, but his rule will end as soon as a new alliance becomes stronger than his. We see through the character of Col. Mebratu that the emperor's 'team' is tested a number of times.

- When Marion arrives at Our Lady of Perpetual Succour in America, he finds an ethnically diverse medical staff united by their shared enthusiasm for the game of cricket. In both medicine and cricket, this group of strangers must trust and rely on each other.

Regret and Redemption

- Everyone in this novel, as in life, makes mistakes. Each character regrets some of the choices he or she has made. *"You live [life] forward, but understand it backward. It is only when you stop and look to the rear that you see the corpse caught under your wheel."* (p.9)

- Confession is one route by which acknowledgement tries to achieve redemption, but this is not the full sense that Verghese presents. He understands that confession is not only about admission, but is about self and public acknowledgement. Whether confession will bring relief or redemption is seen differently in different characters.

- o Matron's story about John Melly allows Ghosh to see her as a full human being. She regrets his death and dedicated herself to Ethiopia in his memory. Her disclosure was a personal recognition of what she owed someone she loved.
- o Thomas Stone's story, told in Marion's presence, was not so much justification of his relationship with Sister Mary Joseph Praise, but an airing of all he had locked inside for so many years. Once his remorse was out in the open, Stone could start to fill in the emotional holes in his life, one small step at a time.
- o It is Genet's confession that is missing the regret and remorse that she owes Marion for nearly destroying his life. She is not redeemed by her confession, but frees Marion to seek his own path to reclaiming and redeeming his life.
- o Even Ghosh has some regrets at the end of his life. He wished he could have been a better friend to Thomas Stone. But wishing and hoping does not guarantee success. At times, we choose a path that leads us away from our goal. Ghosh's story of the slippers is a reminder to accept our choices and our nature, rather than fight or regret what we are. (see Slippers, p.54)

- Redemption can heal regrets and renew hope. Some characters seek redemption in religion (e.g., Matron and Sister Mary Joseph Praise), some in medicine (e.g., Missing Hospital's patients and doctors), some in politics (e.g., Zemui and Mebratu), and some try different sources at different times.

Consider regret and redemption in relation to Shiva, Marion, the Probationer, Tsige, and others.

WRITING STYLE AND STRUCTURE

Narration

Framing Device

Plot

Style

WRITING STYLE AND STRUCTURE

Narration

- The novel opens in the first-person voice of Marion Praise Stone. Although he remains the narrator all the way through, his story quickly expands beyond his own voice and viewpoint.

- Many events are described which Marion did not witness, from the third-person viewpoint of a character who was there. These scenes include the thoughts and emotions of the point-of-view character: *"The probationer's heart hammered against her breast like a moth in a lamp."* (p.100) *"That, [Hema] said to herself, is visceral pain. As angry as she'd been with him, the depth of his grief and shame moved her."* (p.125)

Framing Device

- In the Prologue, Marion as narrator introduces this book as his personal history, the results of his quest to learn about his background. This approach allows him (i.e. Verghese) to tell some parts of the story as Marion, and also to step back and let Matron, Hema, Ghosh, and others make contributions. We get to know these characters more intimately by seeing events through their eyes, than if the whole story were presented as Marion sees it.

- All of Part One is Marion's narration of his own birth. This is an unusual and intriguing opening because it forces Marion to draw on the memories of others. Thus he sets up the book's strategy of changing viewpoints, and detouring into other characters' recollections about their own lives.

Plot

- The main plot is Marion's life story, but his frequent narrative hand-offs to other characters echo the team spirit we see among the doctors in a hospital and the cricket players in a game. Sometimes, the story stays in the same scene but shifts to a different character's viewpoint. More often, with a new viewpoint comes a new story line.

- Like blood vessels, all of the book's storylines keep energy pumping through the same core narrative. Jumping from one to another maintains tension and suspense, as we leave a drama in progress without knowing how it will resolve.

- The various story lines converge in the beginning in operating theatre number 3. In the end, they converge again during ShivaMarion's operation.

Storyline

- The writing is sensory, visual, full of description and detail. In addition to the narrator's comments about what Missing Hospital looks like (p.3,4) or how it feels to arrive in New York City (p.461,462), it includes other characters' perceptions of places: Ghosh doing errands in downtown Addis Ababa (p.143-153), Matron showing a patron around the hospital (p.189-191).

- Verghese's style is complex enough to convey emotions and ideas while remaining accessible. He often creates suspense by giving a part or preview of a plot development which will unfold more fully at a later point in the book. In the prologue, for instance, we learn that Marion and Thomas Stone will unite to do surgery together, but we don't know how that will happen — or that the patient will be Shiva.

- This book is full of information, i.e. about medical practices, Ethiopian customs and locales, and cricket, making it instructive as well as enjoyable.

- Unfamiliar material enriches the story: references to places most readers have never seen, objects and rituals most have never heard of. Some of these are explained, while others simply add depth and color to the narrative. *"[Hema] was surprisingly graceful and light on her feet, the neck and head and shoulder gestures of Bharatnatyam automatic for her ... Outside the hospital, as the light faded, the lions in the cages near the Sidist Kilo Monument, anticipating the slabs of meat the keeper would fling through the bars, roared with hunger and impatience; in the foothills of Entoto, the hyenas heard and paused ..."* (p.130)

- Some of the characters' ideas are expressed with sophistication, others in truisms which border on clichés. *"When Gebrew met us at the gate and said men had come and snatched Ghosh from Missing, my childhood ended. I was twelve years old, too old to cry, but I cried for the second time that day because it was all I knew to do."* (p.312)

Cliches are familiar thoughts that readers relate to, which makes the book's content readily accessible.

Symbols

This is a book rich in symbols. The resonance of recurring motifs echoes the power of ritual and religious belief in the surrounding culture. *"Life is full of signs,"* says Marion. *"The trick is to know how to read them."* (p.419)

Blood

- According to the dictionary, lifeblood is the indispensible factor or influence that gives something its strength and vitality. It is the essence of life. Blood, as a symbol, is connected to the characters and to the life of the story. (see Hema, p.25)

- Shiva dies from unstoppable bleeding in his brain, from a lifelong malformation no one knew he had. This *"spider knot of vessels"* may have come from his prebirth link to Marion, or from his father's attempt to kill him before birth in order to save his mother's life.

- When Hema charges into the operating room where Sister Mary Joseph Praise is dying, her eyes are bloodshot. She severs the fleshy stem linking the twins, from which they are bleeding to death.

- Hema also calls for blood to save the mother's life. Blood at Missing Hospital is donated by the staff to save patients' lives. Many patients refuse to give blood, which (literally as well as symbolically) represents both life and death, as well as injury and suffering.

- "Bloody" is a strong curse word in England and its former colonies, including India. When Hema calls the pilot who almost crashed her plane a bloody mercenary, he is outraged: *"He seemed to take far more exception to 'bloody' than 'mercenary.'"* (p.78)
- Blood is shed in the name of love, life, death, and politics. Bad blood can be linked to the breaking of promises, which can, in turn, be reconnected to betrayal. This can be personal, as it is for Marion, or political, as it is for Eritrea and Ethiopia, as well as for the emperor.
- Again, Verghese leaves no symbolic stone unturned.

Stone

- As a symbol, stone is obstructive and hard, but can disintegrate. It is a perfect name for the surgeon Thomas Stone: hard on the outside, but finely granulated on the inside, he sinks into the quicksand of his own personality.
- In the human body (and many other places), a stone is a foreign object, and should be removed. "Cutting for stone" refers to this kind of surgery (see Cutting for Stone, p.34). If kidney or gallstones were cut out by an unskilled traveling doctor who simply closed up the incision and left, an infection was likely to set in and kill the patient. This is what happens when Rosina lets a nonsterile surgical procedure be performed on her daughter, Genet.
- A stone is also the pit of a fruit. It can represent the center of an action or relationship, or an obstacle. One of the epigraphs to Part III is: *"Theirs is the stoneless fruit of love / Whose love is returned."* (p.221) The stone is the part of the fruit that renews the life of the fruit, too, as Thomas Stone does for his son Marion in the end.

Dance

- Dance enters the twins' lives as soon as they are born. Stirred by the chaos around her, calling on the god Shiva, Hema dances with the babies in her arms (p.129). Her strong emotions, and her communication to the boys, is expressed through movement, not words.

    What a journey ... what a day ... what madness, so much worse than tragic! What to do except dance, dance, only dance ... (p.130)

- The god Shiva is known as the creator of dance, and is often depicted with two sets of arms. For both twins, dance has moments of power in their lives. Dancing is especially important to the boy Shiva — Hema teaches him, and he loves it. It is one of the ways he separates from Marion, as well as a way to express himself and communicate with others. Marion later becomes aware of his sexuality through his dance with the Probationer. (p.375)

- The physical push/pull of dance echoes the push/pull of attraction and repulsion that recurs throughout the book. Dance partners are close at certain points, then move apart. Some of the movements are mirror images of each other, like the twins.

- Dance is also a reflection of joy (and melancholy). Music has a power that reaches out – when Marion is in the U.S. and hears the "tizita," it vividly evokes other places, emotions, and memories. He is briefly transformed by both music and dance.

- A different sort of dance is the childhood game of Blindman's Bluff, played by Shiva, Marion, and Genet. This dance depends on skills beyond sight and physical movement. In Marion's case, he always finds Genet by smell. Different senses offer different perspectives.

- Both the game and dance provide the alternate outlooks used by the characters as they move forward in their relationships and in life.

Holes

- *"According to Shiva, life is in the end about fixing holes."* (p.9) Marion introduces this image at the beginning of his story, and it recurs throughout.

- A hole may be an injury or tear — damage that needs fixing. Shiva's medical specialty is repairing fistulas: a hole between a girl's bladder and vagina, typically from bearing a child her body is unable to deliver. (p.425-427)

- A hole may be an absence created by the loss or betrayal of a loved one. Almost every character in the book has at least one such hole in his or her life.

- A hole may be an abyss into which someone disappears: the motor-cycle thief is sucked into quicksand; Ghosh is taken away by four men in a jeep to prison. (p.309)

- A hole is an extension of what is missing, be it people, history, faith, or relationships. The unseen and invisible leave a space which often wields a real power. This is most evident for Marion who longs to fill the hole left by his missing mother, father, and Genet.

Transplant

- It seems as though the heart of the novel is in the liver. Thomas Stone is in the liver transplant business, but every character in the novel is a transplant of some kind. The idea of transplant is as central to the story as are the ideas of separation and conjoinment, both of which occur in the process of medical transplant.

- The idea of transplant is closely linked to the idea of symbiosis, the interaction of two things working in tandem, like ShivaMarion, as they called themselves when they were young.

Consider the theme of transplant in conjunction with belonging, rejection, and acceptance. Does the idea of transplant contribute to the theme of redemption? If so, how?

Slippers

- Ghosh tells the tale of the man who tries repeatedly, and fails, to get rid of his worn-out slippers. The moral is that the slippers can't be thrown away until the owner wears them out and gives them a place of honor. In the tale, and elsewhere in the book, the slippers represent the personal history that follows every person: if you try to leave it behind without attempting to understand it, it will catch up with you and will become your destiny. This is what happens to Stone and to Genet. This is Marion's motive for writing this book: he is trying to understand his own history.

  > *In order to start to get rid of your slippers, you have to admit they are yours, and if you do, then they will get rid of themselves ...*
  >
  > *... The key to your own happiness is to own your slippers, own who you are, own how you look, own your family, own the talents you have, and own the ones you don't. If you keep saying your slippers aren't yours, then you'll die searching, you'll die bitter, always feeling you were promised more."* (p.351)

- This is precisely what happens to Genet.

- Shiva's anklet is a mirror image of the slippers: Ghosh puts it on him to make sure he doesn't die in his sleep, and Shiva never lets anyone take it off until he finds out that Ghosh and Hema have killed Koochooloo's puppies. His distress comes from the fear that he and Marion could be discarded and forgotten as easily as the tiny dogs.

- Shiva's anklet is a personal extension of himself, as is Thomas Stone's finger and Marion's impossible dream of Genet. For each of these characters, these attachments represent the slippers that were likely to hobble their step-by-step progress toward redemption. They have to let go in order to head down the road to a place of final understanding. (see Regret and Redemption, p.42)

  > *[Shiva] said, "Marion always thought that I never looked back. He saw me as always acting only for myself. He was right ... But ... seeing that my brother might die, I have looked back. I have regrets.* (p.621)
  >
  > *[Thomas] didn't tell [Hema] how, when things had looked so dire in the operating room, he'd looked up at the ceiling and prayed not to a God or to spiders, but to Sister Mary Joseph Praise, asking to be redeemed for a lifetime of mistakes.* (p.629)
  >
  > *...Genet had passed away in a prison hospital in Galveston just as I was regaining my strength ... I'm ashamed to say I felt relief when the word came; only her death could ensure that we didn't keep tearing each other apart for what remained of our lives.* (p.644)

Consider the slippers worn by the other characters. Who will successfully cast off their past and who will not?

LAST THOUGHTS
Healing vs. Curing

LAST THOUGHTS

Healing vs. Curing

- From Hippocrates to Verghese, doctors always look to heal, to fix the broken, and to fill in the holes, metaphorically and literally. As Marion says, this is an *"apt metaphor for our profession."* (p.9)

- This is a daunting task, not to be taken lightly or to be accomplished quickly. Verghese has carefully built his story and themes around his exceptionally well-developed characters and through a complex and layered plot.

- Verghese is not content to just create a moving story, he wants to emphasize that healing is not curing. The challenge is to show how people strive to overcome physical, emotional, and spiritual afflictions.

- Thomas Stone had an adage: what is the treatment given through the ear in the case of an emergency? The answer, as Stone had long ago written in his book, is "words of comfort." Stone had learned this from his medical role model, Dr. Braithwaite, but it took him a lifetime to internalize its message.

- Words of compassion, as an empathetic medical remedy, seems incongruous next to Stone's hard and steely demeanor. While Stone has confidence in their therapeutic qualities, he doesn't know how to properly apply them.

- When Stone ran away, both Hema and Ghosh were angry and resentful. They were afraid that Stone would return to claim the boys. By the time Hema reaches New York, she has let go of her anxiety. Ghosh comes to his moment of realization as he dies.

- Ghosh asks Marion to seek out Stone and tell him that Ghosh finally understands Stone's fears and terrors. He wants to put Stone at ease by settling both his own and Thomas Stone's mind. Ghosh's request is a double act of healing. First, it allows Stone to open up and tell his story. These will be his words of comfort. Secondly, Marion's relayed message will push Marion to start to understand his father.

- As this guide has indicated, there are many themes and ideas that Verghese has put forward: medicine, politics, and religion — but they are all about people and the obstacles they face. Physically, a body might be healed and a country restructured, but in either case, it is the spirit that must be cured. Inner peace for the self and spiritual compassion for another fills in the larger picture of life.

- Verghese, the doctor-turned-writer, is ultimately concerned with the whole patient/reader. He is looking for the cure, not just the healing treatment. As Stone's truism puts forward, a cure comes from a human bond; an intimate, warm, conjoined relationship.

- When Marion tells us his story, he is fifty years old, a symbolic midway turning point in a life. His tale, his disclosure, is how he will heal not only himself, but the rift that separated him from Shiva throughout their conjoined history. Because Marion has symbolically lived half his life, he still has time to attempt to seek a cure for all that has troubled him personally and, by extension, his country and its people.

- When Marion sees his reflection in the glass separating Theater 3 from the new Theater 4 at Missing, he realizes that he has decided his future. He will devote himself to surgery in Ethiopia in the name of his brother. They are rejoined.

- The entire book, *Cutting for Stone*, carries a message of comfort to the teller and the reader.

Suggested Beginnings

1. The first clue Abraham Verghese reveals about his title *Cutting for Stone* is the narrator's name, Marion Stone, on page 6. Not until Part 3 is the phrase "cutting for stone" identified as part of the Hippocratic Oath.

When you first heard this novel's title, what did you think it might mean? Now that you've read the book, what do you think are Verghese's reasons for choosing this title?

2. In an interview, Verghese commented on the doctor-patient relationship:

At one level the patient is a text to decode, a mystery to unravel, and that is certainly important, it's the most attractive part of being a diagnostician. But this is not a natural relationship ... They are coming to you because they are in some sort of distress and you are meeting them because you have made this career choice to help people and so it's a very strange relationship and even though it seems routine, there is nothing routine about it. It's really quite loaded. So after you meet them and decode the text, you are, by your presence, by your engagement, providing the kind of comfort no one else can provide. (Tadias)

How do the various doctors in *Cutting for Stone* deal with this "loaded" relationship? Who cares most about the mystery of diagnosis, and who works to provide comfort? How does Verghese use their pre-existing personal relationships with certain patients (such as Genet, and each other) to dramatize this challenge?

3. "Missing" Hospital is a corruption of "Mission." The hospital is run and supported by people — from America, England, and various parts of India — who approach Africa with a sense of mission, whether religious (Matron, Sister Mary Joseph Praise, Eli Harris), or medical (Thomas Stone, Ghosh, Hema), or both.

How do the characters' different personal backgrounds and undertakings influence their work? How do they impact each other? In what situations do contrasting goals create conflict between characters and obstacles to their success?

4. Late in the novel, Marion Stone leaves Ethiopia for the United States. Abraham Verghese is a U.S. citizen and set his previous two non-fiction books in this country. He currently teaches medicine in California.

Could *Cutting for Stone* have taken place in America, for instance, at Our Lady of Perpetual Succour Hospital in the Bronx? What parts of the story couldn't happen there, or would turn out differently? What did you find most interesting about the Ethiopian setting?

5. An important idea in this book is the difference between curing and healing. Verghese talks about this:

Every illness has a physical deficit as well as a sense of spiritual violation. You break your leg and ... there's also a great sense of, "Why me? Why now?" Medicine has done a great job of taking care of the break, but not as good a job of dealing with the sense of violation people feel with illness. To me, that is the distinction between curing and healing – addressing the body and addressing the soul that's in great distress. (Sacramento Bee)

What medical problems in this book illustrate the sense of spiritual violation Verghese is talking about? How do the characters deal with the need for healing along with curing?

6. Although we know from the beginning that Shiva is missing, we do not realize he has died, nor the circumstances of his death.

Why does Shiva need to die in this story? Is his death a sacrifice that he owes Marion or an act of redemption? Does Shiva's death contribute to Thomas Stone's redemption?

7. Marion had an impossible vision of his life and love with Genet. He dreamed of marriage, children, and a house with a white picket fence. In fact he was a virgin until he met up with Genet in America.

What drove Marion's innocent passion? How and why was he so different from his twin, Shiva, who had no need for romantic dreams and who slept with Genet and others, simply because he had the opportunity? What do their respective actions say about loyalty and trust or about dreams and reality?

8. At Our Lady of Perpetual Succour, Marion saw people being saved who would never have been seen at Missing because no one would have brought them to hospital. They would have been deemed beyond help. On the other hand, Marion observed help given to patients who were probably past the point of survival.

What is the perspective of life and death in Ethiopia vs. America? What does Verghese say about how life and health are judged in both places?

9. Before taking Genet's virginity, Shiva slept with the Probationer and more than twenty others. Being a virgin himself and deeply loyal to his love for Genet, Marion felt quite disgusted by this knowledge. Shiva's response was genuine and seemingly respectful: *"all women are beautiful."* (p.393)

Marion is shocked by this statement. In light of the incident with Genet, consider both Shiva's and Marion's position. Was there a victim? If so, who was it?

10. In his last conversation with Marion, Ghosh encourages him to think about leaving Ethiopia. Marion worries: *"If I left, what would be left of me?"* (p.349)

Is Marion's fear valid? How much of one's identity is connected to one's birthplace? Does this change with time and experience?

11. Science and religion, perceived as diametric opposites, have much in common. Verghese has put this fascinating discussion on the table. Doctors, such as Thomas Stone, who put all their skills and knowledge into the practice of medicine, must at times put their scientific devotion aside and just operate on faith. Matron and Sister Mary Joseph Praise, who allow little to alter their devotion to God, recognize the cracks that can appear in their dedication.

Consider the ideas of skepticism and faith. Can belief or disbelief be suspended successfully? What are the benefits? What are the consequences? Discuss the different perspectives on this subject.

FROM THE NOVEL

Quotes

FROM THE NOVEL ...

Memorable Quotes from the Text of Cutting For Stone

PAGE 5. On the plaster above the desk my mother had tacked up a calendar print of Bernini's famous sculpture of St. Teresa of Avila.

Why this picture? Why St. Teresa, Mother?

As a little boy of four, I took myself away to this windowless room to study the image. Courage alone could not get me past that heavy door, but my sense that she was there, my obsession to know the nun who was my mother, gave me strength.

PAGE 25. Sister Mary Joseph Praise was inconsolable, the brave front she'd put up shattering as her friend's body splashed into the water. Stone stood beside her, unsure of himself. His face was dark with anger and shame because he had not been able to save Sister Anjali.

PAGE 33. Such a crucial gap in the history, especially that of a short life, calls attention to itself. A biographer, or a son, must dig deep. Perhaps she knew that the side effect of such a quest was that I'd learn medicine, or that I would find Thomas Stone.

PAGE 47. Of blood there was too much. She swabbed and dabbed and pulled down on the posterior vaginal wall for a better view ... Matron's chest was pounding, her hands shaking. She leaned forward, tilted her head again to peer in. There, like a rock at the bottom of a mud pit, a stone of the heart, was a baby's head.

PAGE 72. *Daring operations performed in darkest Africa* — that was how the publisher had described the book on the back cover. The reader, knowing nothing about the "dark continent," filled in the blanks, pictured Stone in a tent, a kerosene lamp held up by a Hottentot providing the only light, elephants stampeding outside while the good doctor recited Cicero and excised a part of himself as blithely as if he were cutting for stone on the body of another.

PAGE 97. To Hema's astonishment, Gebrew was crying, and his voice turned shrill. "Passage is closed! I tried everything. I opened all the doors and windows. I split open a chicken!"

He clutched his belly and strained in a bizarre imitation of parturition. He tried English. "Baby! Baby? Madam, baby?"

What he tried to convey was clear enough; there was no mistaking it. But it would have been difficult for Hema to believe it in any language.

PAGE 126. Stone wanted to run away, but not from the children or from responsibility. It was the mystery, the impossibility of their existence that made him turn his back on the infants. He could only think of Sister Mary Joseph Praise. He could only think of how she'd concealed this pregnancy, waiting, who knows for what. In response to Hema's question, it would have been a simple thing for Stone to say, *Why ask me? I know no more than you do about this.* Except for the certainty that sat like a spike in his gut that it *was* somehow his doing, even though he had no recollection how or where or when.

PAGE 147. At Adowa, ten thousand Italian soldiers, with as many of their Eritrean *askaris*, poured down from their colony to invade and take Ethiopia. They were defeated by Emperor Menelik's barefoot Ethiopian fighters armed with spears and Remingtons ... No European army had ever been so thoroughly thrashed in Africa. It stuck in the Italian craw, so that even men who weren't born at the time of Adowa, like Bachelli, grew up wanting vengeance.

PAGE 161. The Baptists of Houston were of late Missing's best and most consistent funders. Matron sent out handwritten letters every week to congregations in America and Europe ... If a reply came expressing any interest, she immediately mailed them Thomas Stone's textbook, The Expedient Operator: A Short Practice of Tropical Medicine ... The book, more than any exchange of letters, had won the Houston Baptists' support.

PAGE 175, 176. "We better start," he said to the probationer who was scrubbed, gowned, and gloved on the other side of the table ... "We can't finish if we don't start so we better start if we're to finish, yes?"

> *A very large incision should be made*
> *– of small ones in such cases be afraid –*
> *The coil brought out, untwisted by a turn*
> *– a clockwise turn as you quite soon learn –*
> *And then a rectal tube is upward passed –*
> *Thereon there issues forth a gaseous blast ...*

PAGE 188. "We have more English Bibles than there are English-speaking people in the entire country." Matron had turned from the window and followed his gaze. "Polish Bibles, Czech Bibles, Italian Bibles, French Bibles, Swedish Bibles. I think some are from your Sunday-school children. We need medicine and food. But we get Bibles ... I always wondered if the good people who send us Bibles really think that hookworm and hunger are healed by scripture? Our patients are illiterate."

PAGE 210. "Look," Hema hissed, embarrassed by his behavior, "the father is supposed to whisper the child's name into its ear. If you don't want to do it, I'll call someone else."

That word – "father" – changed everything. He felt a thrill. He quickly whispered "Marion" and then "Shiva" into each tiny ear, kissed each child, then kissed Hema on the cheek before she could pull away, saying "Bye, Mama," scandalizing Hema's guests before he raced back to the theater ...

PAGE 248. *Will you forget if someone kills me or Marion?*
Those words were formed in the voice box, shaped by the lips and tongue, of my heretofore silent brother. For his first spoken words in years, he'd crafted a sentence none of us would forget.

PAGE 266, 267. [Genet] laughed, a cruel, mocking sound, as if she'd heard these words before. I cringed for my nanny as Genet spoke. "Your *husband*? My *father*? You lie. My father would stay the night. My father would have us live with him in a real house." She was angry, tears spilling down her cheeks. "Your husband wouldn't have another wife and three children. Your husband wouldn't come home and send me out to play so he can play with you." She pulled her arm free and went to get her clothes.

PAGE 306. The morning after that, Emperor Haile Selassie the First, Conquering Lion of Judah, King of Kings, Descendant of Solomon, returned to Addis Adaba by plane. Word of his arrival spread like wildfire, and a dancing, ululating crowd lined the road as his motorcade went by. Throngs took to the street, arms linked, hopping in unison, springs in their feet, chanting his name long after he passed. Among them were Gebrew, W.W. Gonad, and Almaz; she reported that His Majesty's face had been full of love for his people, appreciation for their loyalty ... The university students who had marched through the streets a few days before were nowhere to be seen.

PAGE 323. The bike was traveling at speed now, springs squeaking and mudguards rattling, its weight accelerating it down the hill, aided by our efforts. He'd taken his eyes off the road to find the petcock. By the time he looked up, ShivaMarion was running as fast as it could, adding every ounce of thrust possible to his progress.

PAGE 337. But I'd lost all respect for the Emperor. Even Almaz, always a staunch royalist, had a crisis of faith.

No one really believed that Ghosh was a party to the coup. The problem was — and it was the same for hundreds of others who'd been rounded up — His Majesty Haile Selassie made all the decisions. His Majesty wouldn't delegate and His Majesty felt no haste.

PAGE 364. She asked me for directions. Her name was Tsige, I learned later. I heard the muted, glottic, honking cough coming from the infant slung to her back in a *shama*, papoose fashion. It was a sound like the cry of a gander, and for that reason, I bypassed Casualty and took Tsige directly to the croup room.

PAGE 377. She only cried louder. Someone would hear. I didn't think I was supposed to be in this room. And I certainly wasn't supposed to make her cry.

"I said it! I said I forgive you. Why are you still crying?"

"But I almost let you and your brother die. I was supposed to help you breathe when you came out. I was supposed to resuscitate you. But I forgot."

PAGE 397. "Oh, stop. You sound like a stupid romance novel. You sound like a girl, for God's sake! If you want first shot you better move fast, Marion." She seemed serious, no trace of humor in her face. She scared me when she spoke that way.

PAGE 424. Now and then Ghosh would grin and wink at me across the room. He was teaching me how to die, just as he'd taught me how to live.

PAGE 445. As I looked at my send-off party, I felt such hatred for Genet. Perhaps Eritreans in Addis were slaughtering sheep and toasting her tonight, but I wished she could see this snapshot of our family as it was torn apart, all because of her.

It was time to say good-bye to Shiva. I'd forgotten what it felt like to hold him, what a perfect fit his body was to mine, two halves of a single being.

PAGE 466. "*Screw me*? Screw you!" he said.

My mouth fell open. Was it possible to be so completely misunderstood? His face in the mirror said indeed it was. I sank my neck back and shook my head in resignation. I had to laugh. To think that Ghosh – or Lady Macbeth – would be so misinterpreted.

Hamid still glared at me. I winked at him.

I saw him reach into the glove compartment. He pulled out a gun.

PAGE 469. Louis stopped in his tracks to look at me. He laughed. "Ha! That's a good one, Doc. American medical students? I wouldn't know what they look like."

PAGE 508, 509. Deepak smiled and turned to me. "Marion, I'm not a hundred percent sure, because of his mask; had I seen his fingers I could have been certain. But I have a pretty good idea. You just met one of the foremost liver surgeons in the world, a pioneer of liver transplants."

What's his name?"

"Thomas Stone."

PAGE 523. I opened all the kitchen cabinets and left the doors ajar. I pulled down the oven door. I opened both sides of the fridge. I took the top off the juice container. I opened the bathroom cabinets. I unscrewed toothpaste, shampoo, and conditioner, setting the tops carefully alongside the bottles. I opened anything that had a lid or a cover. I left open wardrobe, chest of drawers, filing cabinet, ink bottle, medicine bottles. I opened the windows.

In the center of his desk I placed the bookmark with Sister Mary Joseph Praise's writing on it.

PAGE 559. Thomas Stone stayed in my room past midnight. At some point he became one with the dark shadows, his voice filling my space as if no other words had ever been spoken there. I didn't interrupt him. I forgot he was there. I was inhabiting his story ... His voice walked me into a past that preceded my birth, but it was still mine as much as the color of my eyes or the length of my index finger.

I became conscious of Thomas Stone only when he was done; I saw a man under the spell of his own tale, a snake charmer whose serpent has become his turban. The silence afterward was terrible.

PAGE 568. I studied my father as I might study some specimen set before me: I saw the smile that struggled for purchase on his face and failed, and then I saw the haunted and hunted look that came in its wake. God help us if such a man had tried to raise us, if he had taken us away from Ethiopia. With all the sorrow and loss I'd experienced, I'd never have traded my past at Missing for a life in Boston with him. I should have thanked Thomas Stone for leaving Ethiopia. The love he felt for Sister Mary Joseph Praise had come too late. She was the mystery, the great regret that he would take to his grave — and he would regret nothing more than not knowing what she said in that letter.

PAGE 589. This is my life, I thought, as my taxi slogged through heavy traffic and inched through the tunnel to Logan Airport. I have excised the cancer from my past, cut it out ... I have been the apprentice, paid my dues, and have just become master of my ship. But when I look down, why do I see the ancient, tarred, mud-stained slippers that I buried at the start of the journey still stuck to my feet?

PAGE 614. By midmorning, Hema knew the whole story. Genet had been ill with TB. But Appleby had his hands on the prison health records and they showed what we had not known before: Genet was also a silent carrier of hepatitis B ... Genet had bled readily when we slept together, and I had been generously exposed to her blood and thereby to the virus.

PAGE 620. "This is a *surgical* problem and you are in the best position to help them, precisely because they were never *your* sons. They never held you back, they never slowed your research, your career." There was no rancor in her voice. "Dr. Stone, these are *my* sons. they are a gift given to me. The pain, the heartbreak, if there is to be heartbreak, are all mine — that comes with the gift. I am their mother. Please hear what I say. This has nothing to do with your sons. Make your decision by deciding what your must do for your patient."

PAGE 639. Shiva and I were one being — ShivaMarion ...

He was the rake and I the erstwhile virgin, he the genius who acquired knowledge effortlessly while I toiled into the night for the same mastery; he the famous fistula surgeon and I just another trauma surgeon. Had we switched roles, it wouldn't have mattered one bit to the universe.

Fate and Genet had conspired to kill my liver, but Shiva had a role in Genet's fate, and hence my fate.

ACKNOWLEDGEMENTS

ACKNOWLEDGEMENTS

"Interview and book giveaway with Abraham Verghese," BookRabbit.com. http://www.bookrabbit.com/blog/interview. April 6, 2010.

Blitzer, Carol. "What the Doctor Ordered," *Palo Alto Online*. http://www.paloaltoonline.com. March 5, 2010.

Brown, Tina. "A Novel That's the Best Medicine," *The Daily Beast*. http://www.thedailybeast.com/blogs-and-stories. February 11, 2009.

The World Factbook: Ethiopia. https://www.cia.gov/library/publications/the-world-factbook/geos/et.html.

"Emperor Menelik II (1889-1913)," Ethiopian Treasures. http://www.ethiopiantreasures.co.uk/pages/menelik.htm.

Grewal, San. "Medical professor cries out for better bedside manner," *Toronto Star*. http://www.healthzone.ca. February 21, 2009.

Habib, Shahnaz. *Tadias Magazine*, "Interview with Dr. Abraham Verghese," http://www.tadias.com. September 9, 2009.

McMurtrie, John. "Interview with Abraham Verghese," SFGate.com. http://articles.sfgate.com/2010-03-14. March 14, 2010.

Pierleoni, Allen. "Author Abraham Verghese answers questions posed by Bee readers," *The Sacramento Bee*. http://www.sacbee.com. June 14, 2010.

Thompson, Bob. "Diagnosis: Author," *Washington Post*. http://www.abrahamverghese.com/interviews2009.asp. February 16, 2009.

Wagner, Erica. "Doctors and Sons," *The New York Times Sunday Book Review*. http://www.nytimes.com/pages/books/review. February 6, 2009.